HAUS CURIOSITIES

Breaking Point

For William Podmore, a great teacher

ABOUT THE AUTHOR

Gary Gibbon has been Political Editor of Channel 4 News since 2005. He has won two Royal Television Society awards (one jointly with Jon Snow for revealing the Attorney General's legal opinion on Iraq), and was nominated for a third for his coverage of the 2015 General Election. After his education at the John Lyon School, Harrow and at Balliol College, Oxford, he began a career in broadcast journalism.

Gary Gibbon

BREAKING POINT

The UK Referendum on the EU and its Aftermath

HAUS
CURIOSITIES

First published by Haus Publishing
70 Cadogan Place
London SW1X 9AH
www.hauspublishing.com

Copyright © Gary Gibbon, 2016

The right of the author to be identified as the author
of this work has been asserted in accordance with
the Copyright, Designs and Patents Act 1988

A CIP catalogue record for this book is
available from the British Library

ISBN: 978-1-910376-62-1
ISBN: 978-1-910376-67-6

Typeset in Garamond by MacGuru Ltd

Printed in Spain

Contents

Introduction

Look through the National Security Strategy and Strategic Defence and Security Review of 2015 and you see a recurring theme, a central presumption of Britain's role in the world that has permeated foreign policy through the whole post-war period. Britain's moral purpose, its sense of identity, is to be a force for stability in the world.

Not any more.

On 23 June 2016, the UK voted to cast aside the central international relationship of its day-to-day politics, some forty-three years after it first signed up to pool sovereignty with the Common Market.

Seismic political change doesn't happen very often and it takes a long time to work out its true significance. We are still in the foothills of knowing the full impact of the 2008 Banking Crisis. Each year, each month, another ripple effect is revealed and we get a better idea of the true scale of the original events.

So with 23 June.

I write this in Berlin as Theresa May makes her first overseas visit as Prime Minister to meet Chancellor Merkel. A conversation now begins on what Britain wants to become post Brexit, with some bafflement in Germany that we hadn't worked that out before we voted to leave the EU.

The conversation in liberal circles rampant in the UK in recent weeks has been much more focused on what we have left behind. Since the vote, there's been a mournful threnody of pain from those who wish we were staying in. Paul Theroux once wrote: "Travel is only glamorous in retrospect." The same, it has seemed in recent weeks, could be true of EU membership. There's been an outpouring of grief for something which few had previously shown a deep attachment. But some deep flaws in the international club we have left helped to make this moment possible.

They were vivid and clear to Dominic Cummings, the guiding force behind the Vote Leave campaign, when I spoke to him back in December 2015 while we were sitting having coffee on the terrace of St Ermin's Hotel in Westminster. Mr Cummings told me that Michael Gove would probably never betray his friend David Cameron and come over to the Leave side as he placed too much attachment to loyalty. It was at this exact location 7 months later that Boris Johnson would crash out of the leadership contest to succeed David Cameron after Michael Gove decided he wasn't going to run his campaign after all but was going to run himself as candidate.

Dominic Cummings' central point back in late 2015 was that in the 1970's Europe was something to aspire to, a better performing economy and a more stable polity. It was the shiny, enviable BMW to the UK's rusting and spluttering British Leyland rust-heap. Now, he said, a Briton looking across the Channel would see a continent in a mess. The Eurozone crisis wasn't at its most febrile, but its inherent problems had been patched up and not fixed. Austerity was building resentment and feeding populism in southern Europe. The refugee crisis spurred by the Syrian tragedy had shown Europe had precious little outer-border security and was open to massive waves of people in search of a better life.

The third creation of the EU, the Single Market, was in better condition, but what an intangible benefit to set against the very audible creaking failure of its other two great pieces of supranational machinery. There had never been a better time to take on the Leviathan, Mr Cummings thought.

Britons didn't seek out the role of being a destabilising force in the world but, it seems, they had grown tired and frustrated with the constraints of looking outwards. In June 2016, something snapped. The voters, just over half of them at least, lashed out against the prevailing view of the establishment, discarded its warnings and the advice of allies from the United States to Germany, and chose a very different direction. Theresa May is here in Germany in the second week of her premiership, still exploring what it is that the British people were trying to say and what solutions can unite the two halves of a deeply divided Britain. On my way out here yesterday, a senior Whitehall official told me that, right now, the Brexit plan is "a completely blank sheet of paper". No wonder Chancellor Merkel acknowledged in the meeting with Mrs May that Britain might need some time to sort itself out.

Reporting for Channel 4 News, I glimpsed some of the tensions that exploded in that referendum vote. I visited areas dominated by white, working-class citizens where Remain voters were an endangered species. Many who turned out to vote in these communities were not regular voters. But on June 23rd, they made the effort and they made the difference, driven to the polling stations by anger, a sense of injustice, grievance.

Recalling the Suez Crisis many years later, Lord Franks said: "It was like a flash of lightening on a dark night. What it did was to light up an unfamiliar landscape ... everything was different from then on ... a great many people in Britain perceived at that point of time that what they might have thought before was no longer valid."[1] The EU Referendum was a similar flash of light.

On the surface, just a year before, the British electorate was reverting to type in the general election, doing what it has so often done, electing a Tory majority government. But only 24% of the total eligible electorate voted for the Tories. Beneath the surface things were stirring, core votes were fracturing, new political forces were emerging and disenchantment was growing.

On the morning of 16th June, Nigel Farage stood in front of a poster showing refugees, mainly Muslims, walking through Slovenia, most probably heading for Germany. The caption on the poster was: "Breaking Point". It stoked the fires of anger over immigration and doused a bit of petrol on them for good measure. The specific impact this poster had has been challenged by Nigel Farage amongst others. It was only a short while in the headlines before news of the murder of Jo Cox MP, later that same day, supplanted it. But it captured a campaign that seemed to be going outside the normal rules of political exchange and importing a more aggressive rhetoric into mainstream British politics than we had known. Two parts of the country were shouting over each other with growing rage and utter incomprehension as Britain was approaching a breaking point with Europe and something was cracking inside the nation itself.

How did we get here? How much instability will the vote generate? How much does it show Britain has changed? How much does it foreshadow more change to come? Are the forces that upturned the establishment view in June capable of being satisfied? How far will the ripples extend across Europe or beyond?

While Berlin and other capitals look on in despair, as the demolition dust still swirls in the immediate aftermath of the referendum, all we can really do is start asking the questions and ponder what drove the UK to this moment: not only breaking point for our membership of the EU, but maybe for much else we are used to as well.

Gary Gibbon
Berlin
20 July 2016

Diary, 31 May–23 June

31 May

Two polls out tonight which match Vote Leave's own thinking that "things have moved our way". They argue that the start of purdah means they've been able to get the debate onto their terms. They've said "fuel bills will fall", all part of a "government in waiting" strategy. One former Special Adviser working inside Vote Leave HQ says that Dominic Cummings sits there "like he's already Jeremy Heywood and Ed Llewellyn combined, mapping out what he'll do when he's in No. 10".

It's a sign of how the Vote Leave team has gone for total warfare against David Cameron. "They started it," one prominent spokesman said. "It was their choice not ours." They have to use their best lines of attack, they argue, when David Cameron is mercilessly deploying his. That means going for David Cameron, diminishing his authority where necessary. It also means going for him on immigration and trust. How on earth do you put a party back together again after that?

1 June

One of the top handful of people in the Remain campaign admits they've been "ambushed" by Leave. The "Government in waiting" routine has gifted them the top of bulletins and

Leave say they purposefully kept stuff back until purdah was started as there was no point wasting it while the government had firepower to dominate news. The "Australian Style Points System" got a lot of coverage and, I suspect, cut through.

There's real worry in Remain that Scotland's voters won't turn out in big enough numbers on their side. The EU referendum didn't crowd out the May elections to Holyrood, as Nicola Sturgeon had feared. The opposite seems to have happened. The EU debate has been slow to take fire and I wonder whether the poorer, traditional Labour-supporting SNP recruits who backed Nicola Sturgeon in May and in the 2015 General Election can be quite as animated to back her over the EU.

Late in the day, the Remain camp is trying to get Labour centre stage, to stop this "looking like an Eton prize fight" (as one Remain business leader said on the this morning's campaign phone conference).

2 June

The Tory Remain voices are stilled to give Jeremy Corbyn centre stage. At a London institute packed with enthusiastic supporters he then attacks "the hype and histrionic claims" made by both sides in the referendum. He attacked the draft trade treaty with the US. Listing the virtues of the EU he started with environmental protections, cleaner beaches and the protection of bees. "Oh my God, we cleared a path and he shat on it," were the thoughts of a Tory minister.

6 June

Yesterday I was in the Vote Leave headquarters. Desks of Tories beavering away at maps, data, briefing sheets. Every face I recognised has worked at Conservative HQ or as a Special Adviser to a Tory Minister. This referendum is like a Tory pub brawl that has spilled out into the street ... or maybe a port-fuelled dinner party. I was there to interview Liam Fox who said the government was straining constitutional propriety to breaking point using Whitehall to help the Remain side and stopped short only of illegal acts.

An MP close to George Osborne told me the Party won't fall apart if Remain wins because the 2015 cohort of Tory MPs is a sizable chunk of the Party and will want to get on with the rest of their lives. Few of them live for Europe in the way older generation MPs like Sir Bill Cash do. He insisted that Vote Leave's focus on immigration was proof the Remain side had "boxed them in" on the economic arguments.

7 June

One Remain campaigner said this morning: "We are starting to get to panic stations." To try to cut through to voters still not paying attention to his message, David Cameron's team summoned us to listen to him on top of a buildling next door to The Savoy Hotel. A preppy-looking American family wandered on and off their hotel balcony taking photos of the scene below. Mr Cameron effectively said his own ministers who were on the Leave side were telling "total untruths to con the people", speaking "nonsense" and showing "complacency" about other people's jobs. It felt like a very late addition to the grid, a bit like they were scrambling around for impact and cut-through.

8 June

My memory of Scotland's referendum in September 2014 is that in the final phase of the referendum something happened in the media coverage. For the 'No' campaign it was like a parting of the Red Sea. Their messages were granted top billing in the bulletins and the remorseless gloom about the threats to jobs and the Scottish economy pierced through like never before. Whether it was subconscious bias by the media or simply strength of late-fired material by the No camp, it had an impact. I wonder if something similar will happen on the EU. Remain could probably do with it.

Will Straw of the Remain camp tells me the fundamentals are where they were, people will prioritise economic well-being over immigration when it comes to it. He says if turnout is between 55% to 70% "we are ok". I asked if there was underlying data that was alarming. "No absolutely not." If he's terrified he is very good at hiding it.

9 June

A morning spent in West Bromwich talking to Labour identifiers. We wanted to test the thesis that Labour's natural supporters don't know which side the party is backing. Remain strategists say it's their biggest worry. On the basis of these chats in the street they should be very worried. UKIP got 20% of the votes in the General Election round here. Local Labour sources say they think it could be 60% for Leave in the referendum. In our random chats in the street we found nearly 90% of Labour leaners thought Labour was for Leave. The fact that Tories as high profile as the PM were so identified with Remain could be the central cause. Labour would say it wasn't getting air time for its big name pro-Remain voices. But you can't dismiss the idea that when the party's been 6 years in opposition the Labour voices aren't as big as they were and even if Jeremy Corbyn connected well with voters around here (and it's far from clear he does) his "Vote Remain" message is so qualified you would do well to spot it.

I spoke to Mr Corbyn just before he visited a Sikh temple in West Bromwich. When I told him how voters didn't know which side Labour was on he said: "I find that very surprising."

The Remain HQ is pulling its hair out and he comes across as a bit like Bill Bailey in Black Books when he swallows The Little Book of Calm.

13 June

In Birmingham and Walsall to follow "Labour In" campaign. One MP supporting the cause says they've "given up" on some areas, "we don't go into the white working-class wards here... there's no point." So we dipped out of the official campaign to visit Coalpool, an inter-war estate with much higher white electorate than neighbouring wards. No one here had received any campaign messages from Labour over the course of the referendum. No one we met was voting Remain. Even if Remain were to win, what on earth happens to Labour support when it has merrily gone in a different direction to the MP in such strong numbers?

15 June

Am on a train to Lowestoft. Today the government tried to take back the microphone after letting Labour have two days on the stage to communicate with its voters. That was not considered a resounding success.

Jeremy Corbyn doesn't do the 'stare down the barrel of the lens', 'date with destiny', 'hands on hips' stuff that David Cameron does. But the last two days have exposed a bigger problem for Labour. Who are the accepted icons of the past? Is the party actually too frightened to do a big push in its own heartlands for risk of alienating voters already disenchanted with the Party?

An extraordinary encounter earlier in Westminster with one of the central backroom figures in Vote Leave. I asked if support was straying into any new cohorts? "Absolutely not," he said. "Our people are the old, the badly educated and the poor." He said: "I never used to think this but now I think we can win on any turnout figure if it is 50/50 in the country because our people will turn out and theirs won't."

I'm on my way to interview one of the Oxford graduates who has put themselves at the front of that army of supporters, Boris Johnson. My Vote Leave source said: "Gove and Boris are saying stuff that Farage would and does but they're saying it differently, it gives people the comfort to back (us) ... yes we deliver it indirectly through the messages about (the over-crowded) NHS and schools but a lot of the language is pretty identical." I asked why the Leave campaign was pushing the Australian-style points system when it seemed to be uniquely irrelevant to the UK's particular situation. He said: "It's just a phrase that works with people." Because it sends out a subliminal message? "Yes, of course," he said. "In the same way that 'Swedish schools' was good for messaging for Michael Gove's 'free schools' push conveying a reasonable, liberal country." Focus grouping had hit upon a phrase that tempted some white, working-class voters with an image of predominantly white Australia.

I still think Remain will win this because of the tradition of voters pulling back from the brink. Doesn't a Leave victory require something very big and identifiable to have happened since the 2015 General Election? Also I'm not sure the polls have sorted out their problems getting to "harder to reach" pro-status quo voters. Nonetheless, I've spent some of this train journey tapping out a David Cameron obituary. He'd be gone before breakfast if it's Leave.

16 June

To a fish processing plant in Lowestoft to follow Boris Johnson campaigning. Pro-Leave supporters outside are quite adamant they want Boris Johnson to take over as Prime Minister. In Cromer in the sunshine you see only adulation and support. As we are about to interview him on the pier a sea mist descends with a chill. He's notoriously difficult to interview and this occasion is no exception. I'm trying to read out a quotation from an October 2015 article in which he condemned politicians for using fear of immigration. I keep pressing him on whether he wants immigration down to the tens of thousands. He says people aren't after tiny net migration levels, they just want "control". Interested to see him try that on the voters I've been meeting if he gets the chance.

On the train back to London we hear that Jo Cox has been attacked and colleagues in London say things look very bad. By 5pm there is confirmation she has been killed. Jo Cox was a hugely impressive and instantly likeable individual. On the very first meeting you felt you'd known her all your life. She radiated intelligence, judgement, commitment, but she managed to be approachable and funny too. She wasn't waving her principles in your face when you met her. I remember turning to Ray Queally, a Channel 4 News cameraman, after first interviewing her on the Green outside Parliament. We both looked open-jawed at each other and said "wow" in unison.

17 June

One Cabinet minister in Vote Leave tells me he's convinced the "pause" in campaigning will mean Remain wins and Leave momentum is lost. Remain strategist tells me the same. But the Remain side needed to regain ground, to refocus on the economy. This was the period, the last period of the campaign, that was supposed to have pulled back the Scottish referendum for 'No'.

18 June

The sudden silence is eery and poignant after weeks of relentless shouting across the referendum divide. Some still play politics even moments after the killing. The *Daily Mail* has developed an acute and sudden interest in the role of mental illness in politically motivated crimes. It will be interesting to see that continued. The paper desperately doesn't want this tragic hiatus to halt momentum for Leave. Pro-Remain writers are insisting that the language and ferocity of Leave's talk of immigration and imminent disaster, a country at "breaking point" etc., created an atmosphere in which a deranged person could feel legitimised if not directed to act. Anti-immigration has never dominated the political discussion like it has in these febrile weeks, not since Enoch Powell stirred the dockers and meat porters to march in 1968. Both Michael Gove and Boris Johnson have been pro-immigration in private and in public in the past.

22 June

At Birmingham University for the final cross-party "rally" of the Remain campaign – about 300 people there, many were bussed in. When I board my train back to London I notice quite a few of the faces familiar from the crowd heading south too. Gordon Brown makes a point of not travelling in on the "Britain Stronger In" battle bus. He emerges from the university building to blend in with David Cameron et al. coming off the bus. Each goes on the platform one at a time to deliver a speech so (I assume) Gordon Brown doesn't have to stand side by side with David Cameron. Tim Farron does a good turn showing passion and wit. Gordon Brown does some old-time religion. I could see David Cameron clapping his old foe as he spoke of how you can't trust Tory Brexiteers and how the likes of Iain Duncan Smith would rip up worker protections. It reminds you how David Cameron has had to go into all sorts of contortions in this campaign, including softening trade union legislation to get the unions to back Remain with people and money. The PM's aides talk of an 'Alice in Wonderland' change to their press relations as they "now have the Mirror and The Observer on 'Redial 1'" for helpful pro-Remain stories and access. None of this has gone unnoticed by the seething Tory Brexiteers.

David Cameron gets onto the podium in shirt sleeves to show urgency. He boils his message down to one word: "Together." It's really striking how no one I ever test out on this can recall a Remain slogan. Supporters of Leave unconsciously pepper their arguments with "take control".

David Cameron has another go at the generational warning to older folk not to mess up their grandchildren's lives. The bulletins have been given their last portion of soundbites. And he's off.

Even if he wins he faces the awesome task of negotiating another coalition deal, this time with his own party.

23 June

Torrential rain here in London as the polls open. A long chat with a senior Remain strategist, who reckons the Remain victory could be 55/45, with Labour breaking 68/32 for Remain and Tories "worse than 50/50 for Remain". He thinks the suspension of campaigning activity "re-set everything". He says he has never had Remain behind though there were 3 days when he had the two sides 50/50. He believed that the Leave campaign "went for broke" trying to "stir up D's and E's to turn out ... so (they) were deliberately provocative driving up the salience of the issue (Turkey posters etc)." The Leave camp have "massively magnified distrust, they don't trust anyone now. Many Leave voters live in areas where everyone they know is for Leave. They'll suspect some sort of fix (if Remain win). The result will be incomprehensible to them." Scotland, he said, should've been a lot better but wasn't helped by "Nicola Sturgeon calling the Remain campaign 'Project Fear'. The contest didn't have much edge because all the main figures were on the same side.

And then just at the end of the conversation he asks: "Are you picking anything up about turnout?" I spoke to a EU country diplomat who toured the country before the vote. He told me: "People were bewildered and kept asking me what I thought they should be doing. They didn't trust the campaigns and were asking why are we having this vote?" (I've had the same experience. I've never known so many people asking me, as a reporter: "What would you do?" Some people genuinely want any help they can get.) He said: "If there was a referendum in France, the Netherlands, Hungary, Poland, Italy or Spain right now on the same question it would probably be lost." He tells me there's been serious talk in Berlin and elsewhere in EU during the referendum about somehow moving back to the original "Free Movement of Labour" and away from the "Free Movement of Peoples", but that the "glacial" pace of such thoughts was never going to come to anything any time very soon. He said an "emergency brake" idea could come back on to the agenda. He said EU big players were agreed UK would have until Autumn to move Article 50 but no longer if it votes to leave.

I spoke to a senior civil servant at the heart of the original EU negotiations. He said his background was outside London, he sensed things weren't going the government's way. Provincial England had spotted an opportunity to kick back.

At the beginning of the year I thought Remain might get over 55% now I think it will be below that, somewhere in the grey area. Grey, like the day it was decided (in London, at least).

The Path to Brexit

"In all countries, attitudes to European integration are shaped by history: an attraction to 'Europe' was that it appeared to offer every country an escape from its historic failures – defeat, occupation, foreign domination, dictatorship, aggression, civil war. In England's case, the escape was from 'Decline'."

Robert Tombs, *The English and Their History*, 2014, p. 877

"My impression is that if you, over years if not decades, tell citizens that something is wrong with the EU, that the EU is too technocratic, too bureaucratic, you cannot be taken by surprise if voters believe you."

Jean-Claude Juncker, 29 June 16,
European Council press conference

From the beginning when Britain joined the Common Market, the UK saw Europe as useful not endearing. It was a transactional relationship. A Britain in dire shape in the 1970's saw the EU as a chance to be part of something better. The Left largely saw it as a bosses' stitchup but the referendum of 1975 that followed membership in 1973 saw a 67/33 vote in favour of staying in. Most adults of voting age back then had a memory of World War II. It was a very different world. But even then, David Butler and Uwe Kitzinger called the victory for pro-Common Market forces "unequivocal, but ... also unenthusiastic. Support for membership was wide but it did not run deep."[2]

The passionate pro-European and former Europe Minister Denis MacShane wrote in January 2015 in an impressively prescient book called *Brexit: How Britain Will Leave Europe*: "Europe drinks coffee and cold lager beer. Britain prefers tea and enjoys warm bitter beer. All European nations have written constitutions. Not Britain. They are republics and even when the head of state is a king or queen they are citizen monarchs who retire when old. Britain's head of state lives by convention, not a constitution, is head of the official national church, whose bishops are also unelected legislators. One British king has abdicated in the last few centuries but none has retired. Other than Sweden, every EU member state has been invaded, occupied or lived under authoritarian despotism in living memory or has, like Ireland, been carved bloodily from its masters between 1021 and 1916. In short, Britain is not, in truth, European."[3]

There was a cynical quality to the establishment's signing-up to Europe which never left the national consciousness. Remain supporters proudly point to references of shared sovereignty in the campaign literature and speeches of 1975. But John Bridcut's BBC documentary, *Them and Us,* captured something of the establishment view of Europe, when he edited together interviews conducted in 1995, the first with a member of the team that negotiated Britain's membership of the Common Market, Sir Roy Denman:

SIR ROY DENMAN: I was across at No. 10 when the message came in from (President) Pompidou setting the agenda for the meeting. And the centrepoint of it was Economic and Monetary Union which Pompidou suggested we should aim at for 1980 and we saw this. Heath then came in and read the message and made no comment. Then Sir Alec Douglas-Home the Foreign Secretary also came in and read it and he looked across at Ted Heath and said: 'Hmm. I don't think the House (of Commons) will like this much, Ted.' To which Heath said 'Well, that Alec, is what it's all about.'

The documentary then plays Edward Heath's reaction to the Denman quote:

HEATH: Hm. Well that's what it was all about ... and we'd have got it.*

---

* In the original interview Edward Heath went on to say: "... except for the Middle East" (a reference to the Oil Shock of 1973). When I heard the interview clip without that information I assumed he was snarling about Mrs Thatcher ruining it all in the 1980s. The reference to a crisis only months away suggests just how quickly he thought Britain could have become part of Economic and Monetary Union.

In Downing Street, in the years that followed Edward Heath's departure from office, a rhythm for handling EU relations and summits developed which united Prime Ministers of all colours. Margaret Thatcher began the process in her journey to Euro-scepticism. By the time we get to Gordon Brown and David Cameron it is almost planted in the grid. Confect or embellish a point of difference with the EU for which you can show yourself "going into battle" on the day before you head out. Make a firm pledge to stick to your guns come what may as you go into the European Council building. Emerge at the end of a long, sweaty night claiming to have finally faced the mad bastards down and saved (fill in as appropriate) the prosperity of the City of London, the sacred design of the British kettle or some other cause.

There was no space in this routine for any sort of praise for what the European Union might be contributing to the UK economy or any other aspect of our national life. That was thought to be going against the grain, risked making you look a bit soft. The narrative went very much with the grain of frustrated right-wing newspapers who saw the EU as a bothersome, encroaching, interfering and frustrating force whose every instinct was to suffocate national democracies and grow its own bureaucracy. Much has been said and written over the years about how the law-abiding Brits rigorously observed EU laws and even gold-plated regulations when slippery Mediterranean types only went through the motions of compliance.

David Cameron's attempt at a fundamental renegotiation of British terms of membership was a doomed venture. At the Bloomberg speech a senior British diplomat told me: "This is going to be bloody difficult." A vast demand was facing vast resistance. David Cameron needed concessions that would guarantee lower net migration from the EU. The EU wouldn't budge on freedom of movement of peoples. When it was completed in February 2016, the renegotiation "landed", in No. 10 aides' parlance, pretty badly. *The Sun* headline greeting the reforms was: "Who Do EU Think You Are Kidding, Mr Cameron?"[4] – a nod to the theme music for the vintage BBC comedy, 'Dad's Army', a favourite of the former UKIP leader Nigel Farage (he has an encyclopaedic knowledge of the episodes). Unlike Harold Wilson's similarly thin renegotiation, David Cameron didn't have the entire political establishment lined up on his side. Enoch Powell claimed the 1975 victory for the "Yes" campaign happened because: "The 'best' people appeared to be on the 'Yes' side and on the whole when in doubt the British people follow the 'best people', the toffs".[5] Forty one years on, it wasn't at all clear who the British voters regarded as the "best people" and the conventional political establishment was split.

In 2016, from the beginning of the campaign, the media was gripped by the latest chapter in the story that prompted this referendum in the first place: Tory Wars. Michael Gove had decided to back his long-held beliefs and not his friendships. He helped to persuade Boris Johnson, whose long-held beliefs are a little trickier to discern, to jump with him. Labour pro-Europeans complained that what followed was an orgy of lobby journalists' frenzied copy on their shared specialist subject: the ins and outs of big name Tory in-fighting. That, the argument ran, squeezed out the clear, sonorous voice of Labour's pro-Remain case.

There is some truth in this attack and a mighty problem with it too. The Pro-Labour voice was frail, quavering and qualified. I attended Jeremy Corbyn's first pro-EU speech at Senate House at the University of London (14 April 2016). It was, to be fair, his first ever pro-EU speech so this was never going to be a tune he could whistle confidently. Colleagues who'd persuaded him to back EU membership in the weeks after his election to the leadership in 2015 said the process has been "like nailing jelly to a wall". Jeremy Corbyn wasn't familiar with being "pro" anything after a lifetime attacking the establishment, one former frontbencher said. Then there was the ingrained dislike of the EU as a "bosses' stitch-up".

Even if Jeremy Corbyn had sung Europe's anthem, the Ode to Joy, from the top of Islington Town Hall, here was a Labour leader who didn't connect with many voters in Labour's traditional heartlands. And with Tony Blair very damaged, Gordon Brown depleted, other war horses largely forgotten from daily conversation, Labour's disconnect with its own base was a central component in what made the Brexit victory possible.

With the talk of the genius renegotiation jettisoned, the Remain camp quickly grabbed the "Scotland file" and launched third-party endorsements at the other side – acronym wars began. The OECD, the IMF, the B of E, and even the USA! None, it seemed, impressed the Leave voters. Then they wheeled out their Big Bertha: HMT, Her Majesty's Treasury. Surely the voters would be shifted when told that they could, on average, be £4300 worse off a year by 2030 than they might otherwise be.

The Treasury kept this central weapon in the Remain arsenal to itself until it was ready to deploy. There could be no road-testing of it. If there had been they might have realised it wasn't going to deliver the killer blow. On 18 April, along with other political and economic correspondents, I was summoned to the basement of the Treasury to listen to Sir David Ramsden, the same official who'd written the analysis in 2003 for Gordon Brown's five tests for joining the Euro and authored the Treasury's assessment of the costs of Scottish independence, explain how he'd assessed the costs of Brexit. Even cynics acknowledged that, on its own terms, judged against other modelling, this piece of work observed the proprieties of these sorts of exercises. Fingers in ears, the government fired off its great gun and waited for the reaction. Then they waited some more. And then a bit longer still.

By the start of purdah, when all official government munitions had to be stowed back in the arsenal, public opinion had not shifted. Warnings of economic pain had pinged like air gun pellets off heavy armoury. The people, or just over half of them, weren't moved. It wasn't that the voters had closed their minds to all numbers and all campaign pitches. The £350m emblazoned on the side of the Leave campaign bus, the money that Vote Leave said would be available to the NHS if we cancelled our subscription to the EU, got through to people. The Treasury's £4300 just didn't work. It was, one Remain strategist puts it, based on the "obviously unknowable future", it was "spuriously specific", and the Treasury maxim that "the scarier and bigger the number the better, obviously didn't work". It was coming from an unpopular Tory Chancellor in a government doling out tough medicine during over six years in office, frequently and drastically revising its own projected economic statistics beyond recognition.

By contrast, the Leave campaign had been storing up its weaponry for the moment that purdah began. They dominated the TV and newspaper headlines for a week with promises to lower VAT and much more besides. They behaved like a government-in-waiting, and one insider in the campaign HQ said that Dominic Cummings at this point resembled a Cabinet Secretary/No.10 Chief of Staff-in-waiting, firing off policy initiatives for all the world as if he'd already taken over Whitehall.

This is when immigration moved centre stage in the campaign. The Leave camp had road-tested its potential to unlock the sleeping electorate, people who don't often turn out to vote. They'd trialled the messages that would connect and they'd done a lot of this while Remain was fumbling for a strategy. One visitor to the Vote Leave headquarters in January 2016 was struck by how empty they were but struck too by the focus and brain power of the small team of Silicon Valley data analytics experts who were there. They were building up targeting models. Remain bought their rival outfit off the shelf. The Leave camp's Dominic Cummings told me in September 2015 that he was hand-picking cutting-edge brains. History may record they made the difference.

The Vote Leave camp's own barrage in this period included support for "an Australian-style points system" for controlling immigration. The cynicism here is only matched by the acute political grasp. The policy, as one senior Vote Leave strategist told me, was all about sending out a signal to white voters. Australia, along with Canada, is probably the nation most commonly perceived by Britons to be overwhelmingly "white". As a policy, my source said, it had "no relevance" to Britain's specific needs, no particular merit. As a campaign tool it was mercilessly effective.

It was combined with a poster identifying Turkey as a nation about to be fast-tracked into full EU membership and the Turkish people, their dark footprints across the Vote Leave imagery, about to maraud all over Europe in their millions and come to a high street near you soon. As I write, the Turkish government has just killed off a military coup and perhaps many military personnel with it. Even before that failed attempt to restore military-backed secular rule, EU member state vetoes and the Islamist ambitions of President Erdogan had set back the process of EU entry. It was at best fanciful but realistically pure fiction to say that Turkey was about to join the EU. But that is what Vote Leave's ambassadors to the nation said, repeatedly, on every output. One of them, Boris Johnson, is now our Foreign Secretary.

On 16 June, I followed Boris Johnson on his campaign bus up to East Anglia. On Cromer Pier, I quoted to him his own words from his *Telegraph* column last year:

> When a community is going through some period of stress ... they are historically far more likely to turn on scapegoats in their midst. Anxiety is transferred to some readily identifiable group: Jews, foreigners, homosexuals, gypsies ... they become a catch-all explanation for everything that has gone wrong in a society. Your kids can't get a house? It's the immigrants. Can't get a job? It's the immigrants. Can't see a doctor in A&E? It's the immigrants ... people are only too willing to project their anger on to a particular group, and some politicians, alas, are only too willing to assist.[6]

He interrupted me repeatedly as I read out his own words. I said he was effectively heckling himself. He said all voters wanted was "control over immigration" to rest in Westminster. They weren't, he suggested, hung up on particularly low numbers of net migration. But what I found whenever I went to post-war estates in working-class areas was that "control" had been interpreted as "closing the door". Years of stoked-up resentment over immigration lurked in voters' hearts. Vote Leave had tapped into it to fuel a victory. It was a bit like a political version of early experimental fracking. They'd identified untouched reserves of political support. But this was something mainstream political campaigns had, with some exceptions, avoided. Even Michael Howard's "Are You Thinking What We're Thinking?" campaign of 2005 kept things oblique. This was much more direct and was playing with highly combustible forces.

On 14 June, I caught up with Nigel Farage campaigning in Kingston, West London. He said: "When Boris Johnson and Michael Gove started to talk about an Australian Points Based System for Immigration I thought then well, I've been singing this song for a long time." I asked him if this was his strategy? "Completely my strategy," he said. "And the fact they've decided to follow it I couldn't be happier."

A week later I interviewed Michael Gove:

GG: You're giving a lot of people who are marching behind you in this campaign the idea that "bingo – the draw-bridge is coming up", "the door is being closed", you know that, you hear them. But in reality you don't think that will necessarily happen do you?

MG: I think the biggest problem we have is that public support for immigration has been compromised because promises have been made that we cannot keep while we are in the EU.

GG: You said you shuddered when you saw the poster, "Breaking Point". That's quite a private reaction – some people publicised their feelings at the time, you shuddered in private and then when asked in an interview on Sunday you said "I shuddered". Don't you think you should've spoken out earlier?

MG: I hope that whenever I have been asked my opinion about something arising in the campaign I have given a fair and measured response.

GG: Some people would say you've been in the slipstream, here's your poster on Turkey, you've been in the slipstream of Nigel Farage. Nigel Farage says you're on his agenda.

MG: I don't accept that ... we don't choose the issues of concern that the public raise with us in a debate like this. I've been on audience ...

GG: I think you do. You've bought a whole load of poster sites.

MG: I've been on programmes ... and I don't screen or vet the questions ... and it's been striking the feelings that people have in this country and I think those feelings need to be sympathetically addressed rather than dismissed.[7]

Labour MPs were the first to flag up the Leave surge. They were shocked by the overwhelming majorities for Leave in their own constituencies. Some found themselves lobbying for restrictions on freedom of movement in the middle of the referendum campaign. Their own party brought out a much-mocked "tough on immigration" mug in the 2015 General Election campaign under Ed Miliband. The toughness was, as ever, all about enforcing existing rules and tackling employers acting outside the law. But the neglect of this issue, so important to voters in their own backyards, went back a long way. Professor Nick Pearce, who worked in Downing Street under Gordon Brown, has written of how there was "no consistent policy for immigration or coping with it just periods of heightened panic and headline-grabbing tactical ploys."

After the fall of the Berlin Wall, the UK led the push for old Soviet bloc countries to be admitted as fast as possible into the EU. John Major's government argued that it would make the EU wider and shallower, closer to the sort of organisation that the UK wanted. Two and a half decades later, and Britain was at the front of the queue to leave, propelled it seemed in large part by the arrival of hundreds of thousands of Eastern European workers, themselves attracted by basic salaries sometimes six times what they could earn in their home countries.

But the anti-immigration feeling in Britain wasn't by any stretch all about Eastern Europe. The voters who felt most strongly about immigration blurred history's different waves of immigration. In May, I met Muslims for Britain, a pro-Brexit campaign group campaigning in Birmingham. They were telling voters from Britain's ethnic minorities that Brexit would mean they could have a "re-balanced" immigration, tightening up migration from Eastern Europe and relaxing it for immigrants from their own ancestral homelands in Pakistan and Bangladesh. But the voters in Labour's heartlands who delivered Brexit, the 7.5% extra who turned out to vote in England compared with the 2015 General Election, many of them clearly had Asian, Middle Eastern and African immigration on their minds as well when they talked about Britain being "full." The impact of images of the refugee crisis on Greek Islands like Lesbos, combined with reports of Islamist cells operating around Europe, repeatedly came up when you talked to poorer voters angry about immigration.

The Tories in the 2010 General Election and again in 2015 promised net migration "reduced to the tens of thousands." That pledge raised expectations of action which the Party leadership had absolutely no plan to fulfil. Sir Lynton Crosby addressing a private meeting of Tory MPs in the days after the 2015 General Election warned them they would be judged on their commitments, not least on immigration. In the referendum, many voters, a critical slice, felt they were at long last being given a vote on immigration. They included an estimated 2.8m people who turned out for the referendum but not for the General Election just over a year earlier. They were voting "no" to immigration, even though that wasn't the question on the ballot paper. That's why Leave won. What happens if those very same people are disappointed, as they very well may be, is one of the central questions posed by the result.

The morning of the referendum result saw Nigel Farage standing on the green in front of Westminster flanked by an all-male group of UKIP supporters. A man who'd led his party to winning 4 million votes, 12.7% of the votes cast in the 2015 General Election, wasn't content just to crow about his victory. He demanded that the Prime Minister, elected by a majority in that election, should go. Just about everyone in Westminster (with the bizarre and almost solitary exception of Boris Johnson) seemed to know David Cameron would treat defeat like a letter of instant dismissal. But the sight of the leader of a minor party demanding the elected Prime Minister leave office was quite a moment. Several people that morning said to me it had the whiff of a coup about it. In the Leave heartlands there was no such sense of outrage. This had been a successful uprising, a blunt message delivered with necessary brutality to the figurehead of the heedless elites.

But then, over the days that followed, came some kind of attempted counter-coup. As coups go, it was more bespoke, less 'off-the-peg'. The great and the good started saying the result of the referendum should not, must not stand. Metropolitan lawyers led the erudite charge. At one point, one thousand barristers, not used to be being over-ruled by inferiors, wrote to all MPs demanding a Royal Commission examine the legality of Brexit.[8] It had more than a whiff of "do you have any idea who I am?" about it.

They are the two sides in what is now exposed as a deeply divided country. If immigration was, for many, the scapegoat that Boris Johnson, in an earlier incarnation, identified, then the epic forces of globalisation must be the root cause. They are polarising incomes and outlooks not just in Britain but across the Western World; many pots were bubbling but ours was the first to boil over.

The Results

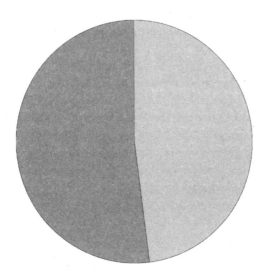

Overall national total

Leave: 17,410,742 (51.9%)

Remain: 16,141,241 (48.1%)

Below are the full results broken down by the twelve counting areas.*

East
Remain: 1,448,616
Leave: 1,880,367
Electorate: 4,398,796
Turnout: 75.7%

East Midlands
Remain: 1,033,036
Leave: 1,475,479
Electorate: 3,384,299
Turnout: 74.2%

London
Remain: 2,263,519
Leave: 1,513,232
Electorate: 5,424,768
Turnout: 69.7%

North East
Remain: 562,595
Leave: 778,103
Electorate: 1,934,341
Turnout: 69.3%

North West
Remain: 1,699,020
Leave: 1,966,925
Electorate: 5,241,568
Turnout: 70%

Northern Ireland
Remain: 440,707
Leave: 349,442
Electorate: 1,260,955
Turnout: 62.7%

---

* You can see a more detailed breakdown at http://www.
electoralcommission.org.uk/find-information-by-subject/elections-
and-referendums/past-elections-and-referendums/eu-referendum/
electorate-and-count-information.

Scotland
Remain: 1,661,191
Leave: 1,018,322
Electorate: 3,987,112
Turnout: 67.2%

South East
Remain: 2,391,718
Leave: 2,567,965
Electorate: 6,465,404
Turnout: 76.8%

South West
Remain: 1,503,019
Leave: 1,669,711
Electorate: 4,138,134
Turnout: 76.7%

Wales
Remain: 772,347
Leave: 854,572
Electorate: 2,270,272
Turnout: 71.7%

West Midlands
Remain: 1,207,175
Leave: 1,755,687
Electorate: 4,116,572
Turnout: 72%

Yorkshire and the Humber
Remain: 1,158,298
Leave: 1,580,937
Electorate: 3,877,780
Turnout: 70.7%

Lord Ashcroft polled 12,369 people after they had voted on polling day. The data below shows the demographic splits and how different parties managed to deliver their supporters or not. David Cameron's failure in bringing only 42% of Tory identifiers with him is a central and sometimes neglected part of the referendum result story. The British/English identity divide amongst English voters shows Leave voters were more than twice as likely as Remain voters to describe themselves as "English not British." Elsewhere in the data, Lord Ashcroft's results suggest that 70% of voters expected Remain to win including 54% of those who voted to Leave. More than two thirds (69%) of Leave voters thought leaving the EU "might make us a bit better or worse off as a country, but there isn't much in it either way."

By demographic

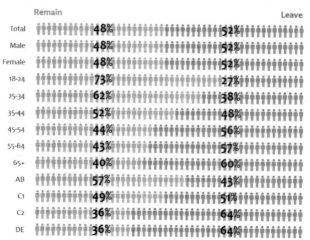

	Remain		Leave
Total	48%		52%
Male	48%		52%
Female	48%		52%
18-24	73%		27%
25-34	62%		38%
35-44	52%		48%
45-54	44%		56%
55-64	43%		57%
65+	40%		60%
AB	57%		43%
C1	49%		51%
C2	36%		64%
DE	36%		64%

Lord Ashcroft Polls

By 2015 GE vote

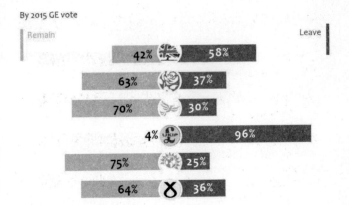

Remain

Leave

42%	58%
63%	37%
70%	30%
4%	96%
75%	25%
64%	36%

Lord Ashcroft Polls

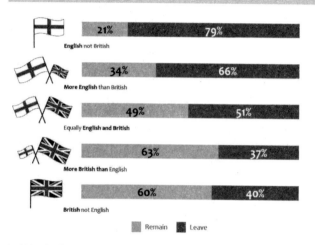

Which, if any, of the following best describes how you see yourself?

English not British
21% | 79%

More English than British
34% | 66%

Equally **English and British**
49% | 51%

More British than English
63% | 37%

British not English
60% | 40%

Remain | Leave

Lord Ashcroft Polls

Diary 24 June–7 July

24 June

The first images and words of the New Britain are of Nigel Farage, celebrating at a boozy party, UKIP supporters shouting "out, out, out". The next image that dominates the screens is the UKIP leader on the green in front of Parliament calling for the Prime Minister to go and praising the vote as a victory for "decent people". More than one colleague suggests there is a bit of a "coup" quality to the images and the messaging.

By 7am I am waiting in Downing Street to watch the Prime Minister's statement. The atmosphere is funereal but you can hear black cabs tooting their horns triumphantly in Whitehall. David Cameron must flip from "campaigner" to "father of the nation" for one last turn in the knowledge that the voters have written him into history as the biggest political failure since Eden or Chamberlain. An entire strategy and alliance at the heart of British political thinking for decades has shattered on his watch. Snappers from the newspapers and agencies talk of "feeling sick". One says his wife said they should move to her home country now. "Where's she from?" I asked. "Kosovo," he said.

Samantha Cameron looks on tearfully as David Cameron nearly chokes on his statement announcing his intention to leave. He says this has been a fantastic democratic exercise, aides no doubt trying to write a better epitaph – they surely know history will not be kind.

Off to the Vote Leave headquarters for a press conference by the victors. But they walk on with stern, grim expressions. Gisela Stuart speaks first. Michael Gove sounds like he's at a funeral and his tribute to David Cameron has a similar tone. Boris Johnson's voice is sandpapered by sleeplessness. He tells the nation's youth to be of good cheer but he sounds shell-shocked. He sounds fearful.

I sidled up to one of the architects of Vote Leave. He said: "Fucking hell, we've gone and done it now."

25 June

Boris Johnson has gone off to play cricket in the grounds of a stately pile. The Prime Minister and the Chancellor are not to be seen. The day after the rupture in UK foreign policy, with questions begging and economic indicators trembling, it seems like no one has a plan. Off to see Jeremy Corbyn, speaking at a hastily arranged event packed with fervent supporters. It's on the ground floor of the building where David Cameron held his rooftop press conference. The purpose is to head off pro-Remain Labour MPs who are after his scalp. Labour Remainers have already started unloading masses of material which they say shows the Labour leader and his team were recalcitrant, reluctant and sometimes obstructive.

26 June

Labour MPs have been sent an analysis telling them that extrapolations from the referendum result suggest they'd be down to 147 MPs if there was a General Election now. (The equivalent extrapolation from local elections May 2016 was just under 200.) Labour MPs will make a move. But can't be at all sure it will work. Everything hinges on whether Jeremy Corbyn is on the ballot paper.

A No. 10 aide says in the end it was "freedom of movement (that) did for us". "You can't have a country with six times the basic income of another, free movement, and not get massive numbers coming in." He said "Boris will win" and "Theresa (May) is utterly brittle and hated by her Home Office staff."

27 June

One of Boris Johnson's most ardent supporters insisted that the *Telegraph* article this morning, widely mocked for its contradictions, was actually "an opening negotiating position". I'm not sure he believed that himself. "'Team Boris is not Vote Leave' is the mantra he repeats." I wonder how long 'Vote Leave' will tolerate that? Kenneth Clarke was putting on a brave face. "At least it's all only a game," he said smiling sorrowfully. His shirt had come several buttons adrift at the front so I discreetly said "your tummy's sticking out". He lent back and shouted back: "It generally does."

I bumped into Seamas Milne in the Commons. "What did you feel when you heard the result?" I asked. "Shocked, really shocked," came the reply. "Interesting," I said. "Others say 'horrified', 'sad'." "Shocked, really shocked," he repeated. "You're really not like the general London demographic are you?" I said. He walked off with his pastry and coffee laughing. An ally of Michael Gove's says that he's lost some of his closest friends through the referendum. "People he would normally holiday with, very close friends. They just won't talk to him again." He says Theresa May has a "Gordon Brown-like tendency ... no decisions are devolved to anyone."

I bump into an acquaintance from the think-tank world who tells me of a Polish colleague of his who was abused in a GP surgery yesterday.

28 June

To Brussels for David Cameron's last European Council. To listen to Remain enthusiasts in the UK you might think a "re-think" on Brexit was a near certainty. They should try a visit here to disabuse themselves. One source here says there was "very predictably" a 'keep all options open' reaction from Chancellor's Merkel's court, but it was closed down almost as soon as it was raised. Chancellor Merkel said tonight: "I see no possibility to reverse this. We would do well to accept this reality." The Poles arrived demanding some sort of weakening if not dismantling of the European Commission, exactly the sort of talk that will strike fear into hearts in Brussels, Paris, Berlin and beyond. Not that Berlin is delighted with Jean-Claude Juncker's Presidency. If it can be achieved without inflicting more pain on the EU it sounds like serious figures would like Mr Juncker to be a casualty of Brexit. There's a tussle between most of the nation capitals and the Juncker Commission. The latter have reverted to the cry "we need more Europe". Many capitals are thinking: weren't you listening?

David Cameron came to this same table in December and tried to kill off doubts about his referendum telling the EU leaders not to worry, "I'm a winner." He's not wanted at tomorrow's meeting. His successor and subsequent ministers will be frozen out of more and more important meetings, their interests now deemed to be very different from those of the EU.

The day started with the European Parliament debate on Brexit. Alyn Smith the SNP MEP got a rousing reception when he called on the EU not to desert Scotland. But Spain's Prime Minister Rajoy, an outspoken opponent of anything that might encourage Catalonia to think it could split off from Spain but still get into the EU, has just got back into power. Would he veto it? He's not the only leader with separatist worries.

A Scottish government source rang to say Nicola Sturgeon was over tomorrow to pursue the point. They are saying this would be different because the mother state pulled out of the EU. Spain and others would see this was different from their circumstances. We shall see. One old Brussels hand said he rather agreed with Edinburgh. Spain might grumble but it wasn't in great nick. It could be bought off if others wanted Scotland in and the thought of a prosperous country applying for membership would do wonders for morale after the UK vote and show the pain of exit can take many undesirable forms.

I asked European Commisison Vice-President Frans Timmermans if the EU would try to punish the UK for the way it had voted. He said, with all his immense charm: "What a stupid question."

30 June

David Cameron told EU leaders on Tuesday in Brussels that the next PM would probably be Theresa May or Boris Johnson. On the way to Westminster for Boris Johnson's leadership campaign launch a statement pings into the email in-box saying Michael Gove has decided he won't carry on being Boris Johnson's campaign manager but instead will himself run for PM.

Tory MPs arrive at St Ermin's Hotel, the Boris Johnson launch venue, looking a bit shaken. Some have already decided not to turn up. When Boris Johnson speaks the normal electricity isn't there. He quotes Brutus in Julius Caesar and then starts running through his past achievements as Mayor of London. And then he says thanks for waiting for the punchline and tells his adoring fans he's not running.

Last night at a West London Tory fund-raiser his behaviour was said to be "erratic". Could it be the awkwardness of sharing a room with Mr and Mrs Cameron? Michael Gove's allies say Boris Johnson looked like "he didn't want the job" almost from the moment David Cameron announced his resignation. Bizarre.

Waiting to interview MPs as they leave, a work colleague tells me his Spanish wife has been jostled and insulted by a racist in North London.

1 July

Off to hear Nigel Farage speak at a press conference. He says he wants his life back and that he's standing down as leader. A colleague who's chatted a lot to him recently says his wife has laid down the law. The impression you get though is of people who created Brexit leaving the stage. I asked him what changes he sees on the horizon for post-Brexit British politics – it's a theme he has talked about in private with the UKIP backer Arron Banks. He says he thinks UKIP shouldn't run candidates against Tory MPs who backed Brexit if there's an early General Election. He started talking about a narrative of betrayal soon after Monday 27th June when Boris Johnson's *Telegraph* column appeared, seeming to soften the line on immigration controls.

5 July

Bump into a senior FCO official. He says the United States is "going through the 'special relationship' stuff in public but is very very frustrated with us" and if we "destabilise Europe, tip the world into recession and prove to have no plan for anything, that frustration will quickly turn into anger". There's a gathering of all the UK ambassadors at the FCO which one diplomat said was "fairly pointless" as "no-one knows who's going to be running the country".

7 July

One of the more surreal recent experiences in this job in what has recently become a crowded market. The Andrea Leadsom "major speech on the economy" (actually a series of slogans delivered to an extremely excitable crowd of fervent supporters including about a dozen Tory MPs) is followed by a "march on parliament". Why, you might wonder, are MPs with security swipe cards that get them access to Parliament on a daily basis marching on the building. The answer is partly a specific message: they want to scare off those they fear are trying to organise a stitch up to keep Andrea Leadsom's name off the ballot paper for party members. But this is also cultural. These are stalwarts of the Tory Right. They don't do smooth, focus-grouped politics. There's something redolent of the US Republican Right about all this, a bit Tea Party, a whiff of Sarah Palin more than one colleague says.

I interview Andrea Leadsom later to ask about her curriculum vitae and she appears to admit she wasn't, after all, in a room with Bank of England Governor Eddie George and few others saving the world from collapse after the Barings crisis. I was told by a contact that a member of Mrs Leadsom's family said she felt she had been spoken to directly by God and directed into politics. So I asked if that was true. She didn't confirm and she didn't deny. She was very unhappy with the question.

12 July

Tory MP Stephen McPartland told me about a ring around of 70 plus Tory MPs that happened over the weekend after the referendum vote. They all wanted to spell out to the leadership candidates that they didn't want an early General Election, many of them for fear of a massive Tory majority. That is how much they rate Labour right now but also a measure of their own divisions. Some Tory MPs felt a new PM would use a General Election mandate to over-ride the referendum mandate and water-down Brexit. Some, he said, liked the influence a majority of 12 gave a small number of backbenchers and didn't fancy washing that away.

George Osborne's front bench career is drawing quietly to a close. Quietly in public at least. Much celebrating behind the scenes – backbenchers are talking about the need to "dismantle the entire court", the patronage system they feel he built up with Gordon Brown-style demands of fealty and a reward scheme that made ministerial office look like an air miles club. One of Theresa May's aides tells me: "We have a lot of parliamentary support and we get the message loud and clear." In the Osborne camp they fear a purge. One MP the Chancellor promoted rang asking how far I thought the purge would go?

Late this morning my phone pinged a diary reminder: Coffee 11am, Portcullis House, Jo Cox. We had postponed a meeting meant to happen two days before she was murdered. Her funeral will be this Friday. What an appalling loss.

13 July

In the Commons David Cameron performs a carefully crafted farewell. This was all about trying to do in a day and a half the legacy managing that Tony Blair lavished months on. And it went quite well, in no small measure thanks to the devestation in the Labour Party. He could mock Jeremy Corbyn, he could talk about his cat. Only the SNP's Angus Robertson lashed him for the referendum, though Ken Clarke pointed up the problems it could bring. Tories, Northern Ireland MPs and a handful of Labour MPs joined in a standing ovation, as did the public gallery. "Look at the public gallery," Theresa May said to David Cameron as he got up to leave, so he waved at them. The Lib Dems were the only other ones standing. Nick Clegg managed the most desultory clapping you've ever seen, his good manners wrestling with his sense that his former coalition partner has wreaked great harm on this country. We keep being told that David Cameron thought he might not have to implement the referendum promise because if he formed another coalition with the Lib Dems after a tighter 2015 General Election they would've knocked it out of the programme of government. But a senior adviser to Nick Clegg told me earlier this year when we saw the renegotiation strategy David Cameron was pursuing: "This is very much what we were expecting to sign off on. We could've lived with it."

Last week though, David Laws told me that the balance of power in the Lib Dem leadership had shifted away from coalition just before election day. Nick Clegg himself, he said, was voicing the view that coalition with Tory or Labour was looking out of the question. Around 7pm I am in Downing Street for Theresa May's Cabinet arrivals. On the doorstep, she's promised a new focus on social justice, strongly suggesting she sees the referendum as a revolt against the elites as much if not more than a vote on the EU. So how do you react to that with your personnel choices?

When David Cameron was trying to advertise the public-spirited nature of Tories way back in opposition you'd get images of frontbenchers working on Africa projects and painting community centres. As I look down Downing Street I see first Philip Hammond, then Michael Fallon, later Liam Fox and David Davis walking up the street. These are not politicians you readily imagine in overalls rolling Dulux onto a youth club's walls. But to Theresa May, grammar school girl, they represent a break from the past few years. I have always found that the Tory Party, in theory liberating people from whatever class they came from, incubates class feeling at a temperature at which you could hatch chicks. It also delineates it with amazingly detailed gradations of hurt and superiority. What Theresa May sees when she looks at these suited men striding so happily up Downing Street is people from her seam in society, people who didn't attend boarding school and certainly not the best known boys' boarding school.

The Cameron team looked down their nose at Theresa May when they first came to office. I can remember one of them saying they'd "wheeled her into the economic team" in opposition when they realised with horror they didn't have a woman in the line-up. The condescension was tempered over the years on their part, never forgotten or forgiven on hers. Now she must shape an agenda on social justice which must go beyond boardroom pay and grammar school Cabinet ministers, while delivering the best possible deal on Brexit.

14 July

On the way home I bumped into someone who served the last 6 years under David Cameron. He said Theresa May had shocked him by her ruthlessness, excising the Cameron clique: "I had no idea she could be this spiteful. The clique has fallen apart over Europe, but it is now on the backbenches and it will re-form." Earlier, in Parliament, one pro-Leave Tory, who worked closely with Michael Gove and the whole Vote Leave team, said: "We weren't meant to win. That line, 'you were only meant to blow the bloody doors off', it's true. The plan was to run the Remain side close enough to scare the EU into bigger concessions. None of us thought we were ever going to win. With the possible exception of Dominic Cummings, who just wanted to drive a car into the Camerons' living room. It's all such a mess. I want a second referendum now."

Post-Brexit Politics

"My Lords, the events of the past two weeks have led to some of the most traumatic and dynamic changes that we have known. The course of the campaign was robust – as it properly should be on such great issues – but at times veered over the line on both sides: it was not merely robust but unacceptable. Through such comments were created cracks in the thin crust of politeness and tolerance of our society, through which, since the referendum, we have seen an outwelling of poison and hatred that I cannot remember in this country for very many years ... It is inequality that thins out the crust of our society and raises the levels of anger, resentment and bitterness. The tools for tackling inequality are as readily available as ever. They are the obvious ones of eduction, public health – we should add today mental health – and housing."

Archbishop of Canterbury, Dr Justin Welby,
House of Lords, 4 July 2016

"The UK that Scotland voted to remain within in 2014 doesn't exist anymore."

Nicola Sturgeon, BBC Andrew Marr Show, 26 June 2016

Politics of the UK and 'Two Nations'

In Downing Street, straight after curtseying to the Queen and taking office, Theresa May declared herself a passionate supporter of "One Nation". The referendum result that had propelled her to office showed that we are nothing of the sort.

Resolution Foundation research suggests the "left behind" communities that have struggled most in recent decades uniformly gave the strongest support to Brexit.[9] English East-coast towns, ex-mining communities, Midlands satellite towns around the main conurbations dominate the list. John Lanchester reflected a few weeks after the referendum: "To be born in many places in Britain is to suffer an irreversible lifelong defeat – a truncation of opportunity, of education, of access to power, of life expectancy". The work they have is "unsatisfying, insecure and low-paid ... (it) doesn't do what the old work did: it doesn't offer a sense of identity or community or selfworth". Their precarious existence makes them a new class, "the precariat."[10]

The periphery defeated the core (London and the South-East) in a way that's almost unprecedented, proclaiming the two sets of economic interests didn't coincide. Lewis Baston, the political analyst, has identified "peripheral towns" that make up "post-industrial Britain" which he estimates have a population of roughly 5.5m. Their turnout was strongly up on the 2015 General Election and only 37.3% of them voted Remain. Mansfield in Nottinghamshire, formerly a mining and textiles town, saw turnout up from 60.9% in 2015 to 72.6%

in the referendum and Leave won in this constituency by 70.9% to 29.1%. Many of these voters didn't believe they had much to lose even if the economy took a hit. 'Take Control' was an astute political slogan to deploy when so many feel deprived of any sense of governance in their working lives. Google the phrase 'take back control' and it is not an accident that you hit any number of mental health help pages. This was a slogan perfectly targeted at the teetering existence of many target voters.

And it sent a stark message and subliminal promise to voters for whom immigration was a dominant concern. David Goodhart has written of how "modern liberalism has a thin and unhistorical understanding of people and societies; it too often regards society as a more or less arbitrary collection of individuals without any particular ties or allegiances to each other ... the 'cruise liner' theory of the nation, in which people come together for a voyage but have no ongoing relationship."[11] Many voters felt their political leaders didn't remotely understand how their communities had changed and cared even less.

Where does this leave a system of two-party politics which has dominated our political system for decades? The former UKIP leader, Nigel Farage, thought for a long time that his side would lose in the referendum. But Mr Farage saw it as a moment to make great gains for his populist cause. He, along with UKIP donor Arron Banks, spoke privately about an "SNP strategy" to steal Labour's votes. They wanted to replicate the SNP's success after the 2014 referendum in Scotland. For many longstanding Labour voters, the experience of breaking from the party line to vote for independence loosened the sullen bonds of party loyalty and pulled them over to the SNP in the 2015 General Election in which the party virtually swept the board taking 56 of Scotland's 59 parliamentary seats. Roughly 90% of Yes voters in Scotland's 2014 referendum voted SNP in 2015. Labour lost around one third of its supporters in Scotland to the SNP between early 2014 and the 2015 General Election, nearly half its vote since 2010. Something snapped. Yes voters "could not reconcile a Labour vote with the position they had taken in the referendum".[12]

Nigel Farage hoped the forces he has led could pull off a similar trick with Labour voters who found themselves splitting from Labour's line on Europe. It might involve re-branding or completely reinventing UKIP, but Andrew Cooper, who ran polling for the Remain campaign, thinks the populist right is extremely well placed to lead an SNP-style raid on Labour's traditional strongholds in England.

This threat to Labour comes at what seems to be a time of wider crisis for the Centre Left across Europe. Social democratic parties in many EU countries are in deep trouble, often unable to get far above 20% of the national vote.

This was, of course, the referendum which David Cameron said would end the divisions in the Conservative Party and settle the issue of Britain's relationship with Europe once and for all. But the results show that the faultlines of the referendum cut through the Tories' support just as it does through Labour's. Theresa May clearly wanted to settle some Brexit supporters' worries with her appointment of Leavers David Davis, Liam Fox and Boris Johnson to her Cabinet, but many in her Party are watching her every move sceptically and closely. There is no rule that says a dominant party of the Centre Left versus a dominant party of the Centre Right will always be the central dynamic in political life. Way before the Banking Crisis, experts detected the decline of mainstream 'catch-all' political parties which had come adrift from their roots and their replacement with 'cartel' parties, based on citizen resistance, populism or nationalism.[13]

Our party political system could soon look very different, and just because Labour could be the first casualty does not mean that the Conservatives are safe from all change.

Politics of UK and its Nations

The moment she became Prime Minister, Theresa May said in Downing Street that the union of the UK was "very, very precious". The day after appointing her Cabinet she flew to Scotland. But what cards does she hold to placate a frustrated electorate that voted 62/38 in favour of Remain and how does she out-smart an extremely canny SNP leadership?

Theresa May has let it be known in private that she was unimpressed by the way David Cameron let the SNP have, as she saw it, a referendum on independence in 2014 on the SNP's terms. It was, she's told people in private, too prolonged, shouldn't have had the Yes/No options and that she would be extremely resistant to granting another one.

Scotland's First Minister knows there are blocks to getting an Independent Scotland back into the EU, with the newly re-elected Spanish Prime Minister Rajoy prime among them. But Edinburgh seems to be looking at the options much more carefully and can spare more of the brightest and best officials to do so than an over-stretched London, distracted by Brexit and its economic consequences.

The SNP leadership is already exploring the flexibility the EU has shown to Denmark. The Faroe Islands and Greenland manage to be self-governing nations outside the EU but within the Kingdom of Denmark. Could a reverse situation see a similar accommodation by the EU? Scotland is wooing Europe and Europe has recently been jilted. That's sometimes a promising moment to make a romantic move, but in a speech on 21 July Nicola Sturgeon sounded like she was trying to lower supporters' expectations.

Ireland has been traumatised by the Brexit result. The Irish government tried to galvanise the sizable Irish population living in Britain to seize victory for Remain. I watched the Taoiseach Enda Kenny visiting a Gaelic Athletic Association game in West London, pressing the flesh to make the point. It was a sign of the UK government's panic that they let the leader of another country court votes on British soil. It all came to nought. On 20 July, Mr Kenny suggested the Brexit vote brought a border poll on Irish unity back onto the agenda, attracting predictable fury from the Democratic Unionists. It is hard to see how Northern Ireland's 300-mile border with the Republic does not now become a customs border. David Davis, the Secretary of State for Exiting the European Union, has himself said as much. Just before the referendum vote, Theresa May said the return of a physical border* was inevitable if the country voted for Brexit. How do you stop EU migrants to Ireland who are taking advantage of freedom of movement from wandering over the border into Northern Ireland and from there into the rest of the UK? Since the referendum, just about everyone, including Theresa May, has committed themselves to rejecting a physical border, but no one, including Theresa May, has explained how that deals with the problems thrown up by Brexit.

And then there is English nationalism. Defining yourself as English rather than British was one of the most accurate indicators of a Brexit vote. But what is English identity? It is not like other nationalisms. A Scottish Nationalist might resent Edinburgh a bit but nothing like an English nationalist will loath London and, to his or her mind, what it stands for. The common identifiers of someone describing themselves as

---

* Theresa May herself warned in the campaign that a "hard border" would be inevitable after Brexit. Since becoming Prime Minister, on the advice from officials (who haven't managed to work out how to avoid border customs inspections) she has talked of not wanting to "go back to the past" instead.

English more than British will be a sense that they are not doing very well, struggling perhaps. They will usually look at the pace of change and migration and feel it is "time to put people like me first". It is often linked to a sense that life would be better if the clock could be turned back. Five years ago, Peter Kellner delved into the issues and found that "English" voters overwhelmingly wanted their country to withdraw from the world and that international agreements were more trouble than they were worth compared with "British" voters who were much more evenly divided between international-ists and isolationists.[14]

The Labour MP Tristram Hunt has been at the forefront of Labour attempts to get in touch with English sentiment. He's recalled George Orwell's admonishment back in 1941 that England was "the only great country whose intellectuals are ashamed of their own nationality. In left-wing circles it is always felt there is something slightly disgraceful in being an Englishman." But those Labour souls that struggled to find an English nationalism they could identify with are struggling even more after June's referendum. Fintan O'Toole in *The Irish Times* wrote straight after the referendum: "England has not had the time, nor made the effort, to develop an inclusive, civic, progressive nationalism. It is left with a nationalism that is scarcely articulated in positive terms at all and that thus plugs into the darker energies of resentment and xenophobia."[15]

The Union seems to have a diminishing hold on many hearts within it. Theresa May can proclaim its preciousness but those who believe in it need to justify it once again, show its relevance or reshape it.

Relations with Europe and the World

At the EU Council meeting in June, David Cameron's last, President Hollande said Brexit "can serve as a lesson for those who seek the end of Europe". The Dutch PM, Mark Rutte, long invoked as a trusty ally by David Cameron in the years before the referendum, was transformed into a 'former ally' in front of our eyes. He said the sight of Britain falling apart after the referendum would be a wake-up call to EU citizens flirting with leaving. Wishful thinking?

In Berlin for Theresa May's visit, pundits pointed at how some populists on the Right across the EU had fallen back in national polls as their supporters watched the UK struggle with the voters' verdict and the fallout of the financial markets. If they revive and the champagne toasting of Brexit by leaders like Marine Le Pen is justified it will shape the way the UK is dealt with in the exit negotiation and the wider sense of whether this country is an awkward neighbour or an international menace.

A senior figure at Vote Leave texted me the day after the referendum result: "There won't be a vacuum ... we've done our homework ... a lot of time has been spent over the past year informally speaking to EU embassies in London ... it's all in the speech the Lobby dubbed 'the Albanian Option'. That was a reference to Michael Gove's speech on 19 April when he spoke of Britain getting a free trade deal as a base and then negotiating other arrangements on top of that. But Brussels has seen those sorts of "stabilisation and association" agreements as something only to help out struggling and aspirant members.

As politics turned into a Jacobean tragedy in the aftermath of the referendum, all the Vote Leave candidates for the leadership were taken out or imploded. The Brexit supporters who ended up in Theresa May's Cabinet are, with the exception of Boris Johnson, not the ones closest to the Vote Leave operation. If there is a master-file with the answer to the Brexit question in the London South Bank offices occupied by Vote Leave Theresa May doesn't seem to be asking for it.

In his first post-Brexit newspaper column, Boris Johnson promised a nervous nation that British people's right to work in the EU would be unfettered, "there will continue to be free trade, and access to the single market ... (and) the Government will be able to take back democratic control of immigration policy, with a balanced and humane points-based system".[16] He later apologised for being a bit tired when he wrote it. But both Theresa May and the Chancellor, Philip Hammond, have indicated that they want some sort of sliding-scale negotiation in which some access to the Single Market is traded for some restrictions on freedom of movement. In Berlin, at her meeting with Theresa May, Chancellor Merkel was gnomic when asked for her views. In Paris, on 21 July, President Hollande sounded like he would not accept it. David Davis, the Secretary of State for Exiting the European Union, has told allies that Europe's 27 remaining nations will have too much on their plate with the continuing Eurozone problems and the migrant crisis to risk provoking another crisis they can't control and will make significant concessions to the British position. One expert in Berlin I spoke to scoffed at that. Charles Grant of the Centre for European Reform is convinced that the EU isn't up for such a deal and Britain will get a variation of the Canada free-trade deal, with the City's financial institutions taking a very big hit.

In London, on 19 July, the US Secretary of State John Kerry talked of the shared interests of the US and the UK that would remain regardless of Brexit. If, say, Greece left the EU some observers see it as more than possible that the Greeks could make a geo-strategic leap in the direction of the Russian sphere of influence. The UK, the US realises, is not on any such journey. But the Brexit shock comes on top of a recent history of military failure, not least the Helmand mission, spelt out in brutal detail by the Iraq Inquiry Report. On top of that there is a continuing problem of the deficit, potentially worsened by anxiety around Brexit, and there is an isolationist spirit that permeated the Leave voter even if some of the leaders of the Leave campaign proclaimed their cause an outward-looking internationalist mission.

The UK government will feel it wants to prove its out-ward-looking intentions and show it remains worthy of the roles it still holds in the post-War architecture: the seat at the UN Security Council, at the IMF, in the G7 and the G20 and in NATO. The "quiet diplomatic leverage – including moderating European trade demands and strong-arming nations to contribute more to NATO military missions – is suddenly diminished," one US commentator wrote.[17] Admiral James Stavridis, former Supreme Allied Commander in Europe, suggested that Britain, having marginalised its economic role in the world, "will have to look for new ways to demonstrate value in its partnership with the United States if it hopes to maintain anything like the 'special relationship' it has become accustomed to (and dependent on)."[18]

When they were resisting the charms of Europe back in the 1950s, Eden and Churchill preached the doctrine of the Three Circles: Europe, the Commonwealth and the Anglo-American relationship. Britain's position at the centre of all three, it was argued, gave it a unique influence and perspective. A few Leave campaigners spoke romantically of Commonwealth connections in this referendum, but links with former dominions were nothing like as prominent as in Harold Wilson's renegotiation and the 1975 referendum. Lord (Douglas) Hurd used to compare the UK/US relationship to a penny farthing shape. Some in Washington need convincing we are not the buckled little wheel of the penny farthing. Europe will take some convincing we are not an unreliable "Boris bike" with no lights and erratic steering.

The Way We Do Politics

David Cameron's pledge to reduce immigration to the tens of thousands, demonstrating an understanding of the problem by promising something drastic he would be unable to deliver, was perhaps the worst possible way to acknowledge public concern.

The EU's cherished principle of Free Movement of Peoples meant EU migration could not be controlled and the government wasn't about to slash non-EU migration to make up for that. On 26 May, when the Office for National Statistics published the up-to-date figures in one of the worst days of the campaign for Remain, non-EU net migration was even higher than EU net migration, 188,000 a year compared with 184,000.

It was open to British politicians to attempt a Robert Peel moment: to turn to the British population and say (what many of them in their hearts believe and will happily say privately) that high net migration is the price of prosperity. When Robert Peel told the country the unpalatable truth that protection and the Corn Laws were the road to ruin, history proved him right and the benefits to wider prosperity were immense. The impact on his own Conservative Party was devastating. Very few politicians have dared even tiptoe near an equivalent twenty-first century challenge to voter instincts. Perhaps more importantly they haven't addressed the pressure on services in areas of high net migration.

But there are even deeper untruths that run through recent decades of UK politics that probably helped to make the Brexit vote possible. At the heart of a number of Labour and Tory manifestos has been the dreamy combination of US levels of taxation and Scandanavian levels of welfare. When Tony Blair and Gordon Brown promised not to alter the higher and lower rates of income tax, and when David Cameron and George Osborne repeatedly committed to lower taxes, they were not presenting it as part of an American-style smaller state. They were eliding the costs as they publicised the immediate benefits. There were assumptions in all of this about where the centre of public opinion was on taxation and where influential newspaper opinion was too. The two main parties were straining objective truth and the Theresa May/Philip Hammond alliance of "social justice" and "low taxation" looks, at first glance, as though it could do more of the same.

As the forces of globalisation hack away at job security and salary security for many Britons of working age, the need for a more comprehensive and honest approach is even greater. Either embrace a modernised, generous welfare state and raise taxes to pay for it or go for the "Singapore" option of an offshore tax haven in Europe. The only people truly embracing the latter were, of course, deeply embedded in the Vote Leave campaign, the very same people who were promising to splash around any saved money from the EU subscription on that mighty state enterprise, the NHS.

Language and Facts

This referendum coined a new "post-truth politics" in Britain.[19] It captured a quantum leap in the cavalier disregard for facts which Michael Gove then seemed to celebrate: "I think people in this country have had enough of experts." Repeat a clever lie calculated to appeal to individuals' instincts and play on their ignorance of the facts (take the Vote Leave Turkey 'Breaking Point' posters) and you win. The marshalling of undisputed facts and evidence doesn't punch through in public debate the way it did. Trust in politicians and institutions has deteriorated across Western nations, as you might expect, in stressed economic times. But there seems to be something more serious, lasting scar tissue damage which risks permanently damaging political life.[20] As I write, Donald Trump is accepting the Republican nomination for the presidency after surfing this wave of ignorance. Rebuilding trust in institutions is a job for policy-makers, but there are some things that the media and the political classes can do to try to repair the problem.

We are blessed with a broadcast media governed by rules of impartiality. That should give us a line of defence not always available in, say, the US. But the referendum showed that bulwark wasn't as strong as you might think. Some outlets jettisoned challenge and hid behind the safety of "balance". One broadcast journalist told me how his bulletins were strictly, almost to the second, timed so each campaign's interview clips achieved perfect balance in each report. The bosses no doubt thought they were rigorously implementing impartiality but they were ducking their duties, abdicating in favour of a stopwatch.

The Remain campaign complained that if the Institute for Fiscal Studies reported on the economic risks of Brexit, the Leave campaign's flaky rejoinder that it was a think-tank in the pocket of the EU would end up the top of the story. That Stronger In complaint seems to me to have a lot of merit.

What should broadcasters do in the event of coming across an highly disputable claimed fact like the claim by Vote Leave that the UK gives £350m a week to the EU? I remember one bulletin looking very pleased with itself as the presenter duelled with a smiling Boris Johnson over the veracity of the claim. Boris Johnson knew all too well that the voters only heard that there was a net subscription. They weren't bothered what the exact figure was. Vote Leave argued they were educating the public to know there was a net subscription and that Britain was a net donor. But they were doing it with a doggedness that "fact-checking" and challenge seemed to lack the weaponry to combat. They knew their audience better than the media. Working out how you call "cheat" without strengthening the card sharp's hand is something the media didn't navigate well and after the triumph of Vote Leave's strategy surely others will try the same trick. Vote Leave would argue some broadcast coverage of David Cameron's "fundamental renegotiation" of Britain's place in Europe was flawed and fawning and that the reporting of Treasury warnings of the cost of Brexit was naïve.

Looking at research measuring media coverage devoted to different subjects in the referendum is a bracing experience. To take just one example, 0.7% of TV news coverage touched on the implications of Brexit for welfare.[21] But the heavily predicted post-Brexit inflation that could be coming our way could have a mighty impact on working age welfare recipients. Resolution Foundation modelling suggests inflation is now looking like it'll mean that the £600 cut in tax credits lined up for a dual income family with 2 children will become a £1300 cut.

We were, as ever, seduced by process, gripped by strategy, all too ready to tell the easier story of the Tory Wars which for many of us have long been the staple food of political journalism. We are dominated by white, middle-aged males (like this one) forever drawn to certain stories like dated hits blasting out over a wedding party dance floor.

But the dysfunction that meant voters were up for post-truth politics speaks of other deeper issues. Formal reasoning and logic play no part in the school curriculum. If we are moving towards more direct democracy, surely we need to equip voters better to make judgements.

Impartial information on issues like the choices posed by the referendum has never been more plentifully and readily available. It was one click away. I heard many voters complaining that they couldn't "get" the facts. They couldn't, I suspect, be bothered.

Politics in the iPhone age, it seems, bombards the voter with information whilst reducing their appetite to process it.

From the age of mass meetings and church congregations we moved to the age of mass terrestrial television. We have now jumped to a much more individualised or siloed existence, bouncing around our own comforting group of like-minded followers and, critically, getting instant gratification at the push of a button. The 'parleying' from which Parliament takes its name, the necessary and protracted examination of evidence, balancing of interests, the compromises and delays at the heart of representative democracy have never seemed more remote from everyday existence.

The Bernard Crick/David Blunkett agenda of educating our citizens in what democracy is about clearly has a lot more work to do. The lower estimates of turnout by under 25s (perhaps 36%, lower even than the 43% at the 2015 General Election) are telling.

Leaving to one side the fact they could have changed the referendum result, these younger members of the electorate might want to wake up to the inter-generational battle for resources which they appear to be comprehensively losing.[22]

In a column on Conservative Home, before he got a whole lot busier as Theresa May's Joint Chief of Staff in No. 10, Nick Timothy, a Leave voter, attacked the wretched quality of debate around the EU referendum: "Almost all in the entire leadership class feel entrapped by the Political Rules of Engagement. These rules dictate that you can't accept that the opposition team has in any way something like a reasonable point ... total certainty about your proposition is vital."

He and his boss now face the challenge of producing a more honest political dialogue.

But how do you communicate when the voters have their fingers in their ears. In the last desperate hours of the referendum campaign, David Cameron tried to reduce the entire argument for remaining in the EU to a one-word slogan, "Together!" I watched him on a platform at Birmingham University saying the word again and again like a demented British tourist abroad trying to get himself understood in a land where he doesn't speak the language. A gulf has grown up between the language of politics and the language of ordinary lives. It's not helped by some of the technocratic language of political issues like reorganisation of the NHS. I remember thinking as the nation debated Health Secretary Andrew Lansley's health reforms in 2011 that one of Mr Lansley's speeches when fed into a linguistics programme would probably show as much overlap with everyday spoken English as a speech in Portuguese.

Leading politicians might pick up a better language and feel for the issues if they risked a bit more engagement with the public. We have politicians who come from very different walks of life from many of the people they represent. In the 2015 General Election, 3% of MPs elected had experience of manual labour.[23] In the run-up to their 2015 General Election landslide, the SNP managed to widen the recruitment base for Westminster politicians, but it helps if you're sweeping up seats where you've never had a viable candidate on the back of massive surge in support. There's a cocky presumption, repeated by David Cameron in his last Prime Minister's Questions, that frontline UK politicians are much more challenged than their international counterparts. It rests on the quick-thinking needed to take on all-comers once a week in Prime Minister's Questions. Admittedly that's a rare phenomenon in the legislatures of the world. John Major once said: "Most European heads of government couldn't find their way to their parliaments with a white stick." But PMQs hides ever decreasing exposure to all other forms of challenge. David Cameron's team remorselessly kept him away from random members of the public. While Boris Johnson pressed the flesh in accessible walkabouts, taking on hecklers in the street, David Cameron stuck to a tried, tested and controlled format. You stand in a workplace in which the employees have been called in by their bosses to sit in serried ranks listening respectfully to the important visitor and asking a small number of questions under the watchful eye of an employer who pays their wages. Resentment boils up that the politicians don't seem to be under proper scrutiny. And then you end up with the angry studio exchanges that seem only to happen around elections and referendums and which add to the frenzy and the mood of anti-politics.

I think the abandonment of regular long-form TV and radio interviews is also hurting political life. On the advice of his first No. 10 media chief, Andy Coulson, David Cameron pulled out of almost all opportunities for longer

TV interviews (he also abandoned regular press conferences). There are risks to granting this sort of access but it forces your opponents in front of the camera lens too. Boris Johnson and Michael Gove didn't have to face anything like the number of grillings they might have done because David Cameron and George Osborne set the pattern for hiding from that sort of scrutiny. If the Remain forces thought their opponents were getting away with murder it might in part be because fewer press conferences and fewer interviews meant they'd helped to restrict the possibilities for cross-examination. They wouldn't get every voter watching, but over a longer period they could have exposed flawed arguments that would have filtered through into wider coverage.

Most of our front rank politicians were abruptly challenged and defeated on 23 June. They must now find the policies to honour the instructions of the voters and the language to re-connect with them. They will be mindful of the 48% who voted Remain but mindful too that the referendum result appeared to slot a mighty piece of the British power structure back into its accustomed place.

In the elemental "Lord of the Flies" battle for influence on British politics, some of the country's most powerful newspapers surely come out of this referendum convinced they've got "the conch" back in their grasp. The Leveson Inquiry was expected to diminish the power of the press. After the referendum, the *Daily Mail* openly boasted of having won the EU vote and, together with *The Sun*, its role may well have been crucial. Both papers swung decisively behind Theresa May's virtual coronation as Tory leader. They are in their pomp and, no doubt, expecting great favours.

Afterword

Our electoral system has long skewed the focus of our political parties onto swing voters in the relatively few swing seats that decide most General Elections. A referendum is a moment of liberation for the forgotten masses whose votes never seem to count, an opportunity to get their message across. They are the people most hurt by the forces of globalisation and most upset by its most vivid and tangible impact, immigration. As Martin Wolf puts it, "people who see their citizenship as their most valuable asset, forced to share it with outsiders, will react".[24] On 23 June they did just that.

They didn't care that much if Europe's post-war architecture was a casualty of that, they'd had just about enough of everyone else's interests coming first. They wanted 'me' time, attention, change.

The 2012 London Olympics opening ceremony spoke of a Britain that embraced cosmopolitanism, and it was seized on by liberal commentators as proof that their side had triumphed in the culture wars. The gnarled nostalgists and their allies were dying out. The smart, graduate-drenched, diverse cities were on the march. The referendum result showed the cities weren't all marching in step, not in England anyway. David Cameron secured an opt out from "ever closer union" but the ethos many voters wanted to smash was "ever more diverse".

Politicians now face the challenge of delivering a better settlement for "left behind" Britain at what looks like being a time of even smaller resources. They must try to negotiate a new settlement with Europe and relationships around the world that don't make those resources more meagre still. They face the challenge of satisfying the stirred-up anti-immigration demands without damaging the economy, and curbing immigration in a way that doesn't hurt Britain's international reputation. They must pull off this feat at a time when Left and Right in British politics are in flux and on journeys which could mean the British political landscape looks very different in a few years' time. And all of this in an atmosphere of heightened global insecurity and diminished public trust. The Britain illuminated by the "flash of lightening" on 23 June shows us a massive job of work to be done.

Notes

1 Lord Franks, quoted by Prof. Peter Hennessy and Caroline Anstey, *Moneybags and Brains: The Anglo-American Relationship since 1945*, Strathclyde University 1990, p. 10.

2 Butler and Kitzinger, *The 1975 Referendum*, p. 280.

3 Denis MacShane, *Brexit: How Britain Will Leave Europe*, p. xxi (I. B. Tauris, 2015).

4 *The Sun*, 3 February 2016.

5 Interview with the author, Channel 4 News, 2001.

6 Boris Johnson, *The Daily Telegraph*, 11 October 2015.

7 Channel 4 News, 21 June 2016

8 *The Independent*, 9 July 2016.

9 Stephen Clarke and Matt Whittaker, *The Importance of Place*, Resolution Foundation, July 2016.

10 John Lanchester, *London Review of Books*, 28 July 2016.

11 David Goodhart, *The British Dream: Successes and Failures of Post-war Immigration* (Atlantic Books, 2014).

12 Ed Fieldhouse, Chis Prosser, British Election Study, 28 April 2016.

13 Peter Mair and Richard Katz, 'Changing Models of Party Organization and Party Democracy', *Party Politics*, 1995.

14 *Prospect*, December 2011.

15 *Irish Times*, 25 June 2016.

16 *The Daily Telegraph*, 27 June 2016.

17 David E. Sanger, *New York Times*, 26 June 2016.

18 Adm James Stavridis, *Foreign Policy*, June 2016.

19 Faisal Islam, questioning Michael Gove, Sky News, 3 June 2016.

20 Prof. Daniel Drezner, *Washington Post*, 16 June 2016.

21 Table 1.1, Loughborough University Centre for Research in Communications and Culture, 27 June 2016.

22 'Stagnation Generation', Resolution Foundation, 18 July 2016.

23 'Who Governs Britain?', Smith Institute, 2015.

24 *Financial Times*, 20 July 2016.